THE
WITHERSPOON
INSTITUTE

# Marriage and the Public Good: Ten Principles

Published by the Witherspoon Institute
Princeton, New Jersey
August 2008

The Witherspoon Institute is grateful to the
John Templeton Foundation and the Social Trends Institute
for the financial assistance that made this research possible.

The opinions expressed in this report are those of the signatories and do not necessarily
reflect the views of the John Templeton Foundation or the Social Trends Institute.

*Marriage and the Public Good: Ten Principles*
www.princetonprinciples.org
© 2008 by the Witherspoon Institute, Inc.

Published in the United States by the Witherspoon Institute
16 Stockton Street, Princeton, New Jersey 08540

Library of Congress Control Number: 2008935807

ISBN: 9780981491110

Printed in the United States of America

www.winst.org

# CONTENTS

---

*Marriage and the Public Good: Ten Principles* is the result of scholarly discussions that began in December 2004 at a meeting in Princeton, New Jersey, sponsored by the Witherspoon Institute. This conference brought together scholars from economics, history, law, philosophy, psychiatry, and sociology to share with each other the findings of their research on why marriage, understood as the permanent union of husband and wife, is in the public interest. A consensus developed among the participants in favor of sharing more widely the fruit of their collaboration.

The Witherspoon Institute is an independent research center located in Princeton, New Jersey. It is not connected to Princeton University, the Princeton Theological Seminary, The Center for Theological Inquiry, or the Institute for Advanced Study.

For more information, please contact the drafting committee of the Principles at *principles@winst.org*.

# EXECUTIVE SUMMARY

In recent years, marriage has weakened, with serious negative consequences for society as a whole. Four developments are especially troubling: divorce, illegitimacy, cohabitation, and same-sex marriage.

The purpose of this document is to make a substantial new contribution to the public debate over marriage. Too often the rational case for marriage is not made at all or not made very well. As scholars, we are persuaded that the case for marriage can be made and won at the level of reason.

Marriage serves children, women, men, and the common good. The health of marriage is particularly important in a free society, which depends upon citizens to govern their private lives and rear their children responsibly, so as to limit the scope, size, and power of the state. The nation's retreat from marriage has been particularly consequential for our society's most vulnerable communities: minorities and the poor pay a disproportionately heavy price when marriage declines in their communities. Marriage also offers men and women as spouses a good they can have in no other way: a mutual and complete giving of the self. Thus, marriage *understood as the enduring union of husband and wife is both a good in itself and also advances the public interest.*

We affirm the following ten principles that summarize the value of marriage—a choice that most people want to make, and that society should endorse and support.

### Ten Principles on Marriage and the Public Good

1. Marriage is a personal union, intended for the whole of life, of husband and wife.
2. Marriage is a profound human good, elevating and perfecting our social and sexual nature.
3. Ordinarily, both men and women who marry are better off as a result.
4. Marriage protects and promotes the well-being of children.
5. Marriage sustains civil society and promotes the common good.
6. Marriage is a wealth-creating institution, increasing human and social capital.
7. When marriage weakens, the equality gap widens, as children suffer from the disadvantages of growing up in homes without committed mothers and fathers.
8. A functioning marriage culture serves to protect political liberty and foster limited government.
9. The laws that govern marriage matter significantly.
10. "Civil marriage" and "religious marriage" cannot be rigidly or completely divorced from one another.

This understanding of marriage is not narrowly religious, but the cross-cultural fruit of broad human experience and reflection, and supported by considerable social science evidence. But a marriage culture cannot flourish in a society whose primary institutions—universities, courts, legislatures, religions—not only fail to defend marriage but actually undermine it both conceptually and in practice.

Creating a marriage culture is not the job for government. Families, religious communities, and civic institutions point the way. *But law and public policy will either reinforce and support these goals, or undermine them.* We call upon our nation's leaders, and our fellow citizens, to support public policies that strengthen marriage as a social institution, including:

1. Protect the public understanding of marriage as the union of one man with one woman as husband and wife.
2. Investigate divorce law reforms.
3. End marriage penalties for low-income Americans.
4. Protect and expand pro-child and pro-family provisions in our tax code.
5. Protect the interests of children from the fertility industry.

Families, religious communities, community organizations, and public policymakers must work together toward a great goal: strengthening marriage so that each year more children are raised by their own mother and father in loving, lasting marital unions. The future of the American experiment depends upon it. And our children deserve nothing less.

# I. THE CHALLENGE TO MARRIAGE AND FAMILY TODAY

Marriage—considered as a legally sanctioned union of one man and one woman—plays a vital role in preserving the common good and promoting the welfare of children. In virtually every known human society, the institution of marriage provides order and meaning to adult sexual relationships and, more fundamentally, furnishes the ideal context for the bearing and rearing of the young. The health of marriage is particularly important in a free society such as our own, which depends upon citizens to govern their private lives and rear their children responsibly, so as to limit the scope, size, and power of the state. Marriage is also an important source of social, human, and financial capital for children, especially for children growing up in poor, disadvantaged communities who do not have ready access to other sources of such capital. Thus, from the point of view of spouses, children, society, and the polity, marriage advances the public interest.

But in the last forty years, marriage and family have come under increasing pressure from the modern state, the modern economy, and modern culture. Family law in all fifty states and most countries in the Western world has facilitated unilateral divorce, so that marriages can be easily and effectively terminated at the will of either party. Changing sexual mores have made illegitimacy and cohabitation a central feature of our social landscape. The products of Madison Avenue and Hollywood often appear indifferent to, if not hostile toward, the norms that sustain decent family life. New medical technology has made it easier for single mothers and same-sex couples to have children not only outside of marriage, but even without sexual intercourse. Taken together, marriage is losing its preeminent status as the social institution that directs and organizes reproduction, child-rearing, and adult life.[1]

The nation's retreat from marriage has been particularly consequential for our society's most vulnerable communities. Out-of-wedlock birth, divorce, and single motherhood are much more common among lower-income African Americans and, to a lesser extent, Hispanic Americans, in large part because they often do not have as many material, social, and personal resources to resist the deinstitutionalization of marriage. The latest social scientific research on marriage indicates that minorities and the poor pay a disproportionately heavy price when marriage declines in their communities, meaning that the breakdown of the family only compounds the suffering of those citizens who already suffer the most.[2]

The response to this crisis by activist defenders of marriage, while often successful at the ballot box in the United States, has had limited influence on the culture, and in many cases those who deliberately seek to redefine the meaning of marriage or downplay its special significance have argued more effectively. Too often, the rational case for marriage is not made at all or not made very well. Appeals to tradition are rarely decisive in themselves in the American context today, especially among those who believe that individuals should choose their own values rather than heed the wisdom and ways of past generations. Religious appeals, though important in the lives of many individuals and families, have limited reach in a society that limits the role of religious institutions in public life. Appeals to people's feelings or intuitions, however strong, are easily dismissed as appeals to prejudice, unjustly valuing some "lifestyles" over others. And in a society whose moral self-understanding has been formed by the struggle to overcome racial prejudice and promote equal rights, such appeals not only fail to persuade but seem to indicate bad faith.

In this context, we think there is a pressing need for scholarly discussion of the ideal of marriage, defended with reasons that are comprehensible in public debate and that draw upon the full range of social scientific evidence and humanistic reflection. At issue is not only the value of marriage itself, but the reasons why the public has a deep interest in a socially supported normative understanding of marriage. Marriage is under attack *conceptually,* in university communities and other intellectual centers of influence. To defend marriage will require confronting these attacks, assessing their arguments, and correcting them where necessary. We are persuaded that the case for marriage can be made and won at the level of reason. The principles outlined below, and the evidence and arguments offered on their behalf are meant to make that case.

We are aware, of course, that the debate over the normative status of marriage in our society necessarily acquires an emotional edge. No one is untouched by the issue in his or her personal life, and we can readily agree with the critics of marriage that questions of sexual identity, gender equity, and personal happiness are at stake. In arguing for the normative status of marriage, we do not suppose that all people ought to be married or that marriage and family are the only source of good in people's lives. Nor do we wish to deny or downgrade society's obligation to care about the welfare of all children, regardless of their parents' family form.

Still, we think that, particularly as university teachers and on behalf of our students, we need to make this statement, since marriage is above all a choice for the young: they need arguments to counterbalance the dominant arguments now attacking marriage as unjust and undesirable, and they need to know what marriage is in order to sustain their own marriages and raise their own children. Just as it did in earlier cultures, the marital family provides the basis for a settled pattern of reproduction and education that a large, modern, democratic society still surely needs. Our principles mean to summarize the value of married life and the life of families that is built upon marriage—a choice that most people want to make, and that society should endorse and support.

## II. MARRIAGE AND THE PUBLIC GOOD: TEN PRINCIPLES

### 1. Marriage is a personal union, intended for the whole of life, of husband and wife.

Marriage differs from other valued personal relationships in conveying a full union of husband and wife—including a sexual, emotional, financial, legal, spiritual, and parental union. Marriage is not the ratification of an existing relation; it is the beginning of a new relationship between a man and a woman, who pledge their sexual fidelity to one another, promise loving mutual care and support, and form a family that welcomes and nurtures the children that may spring from their union. This understanding of marriage has predominated in Europe and America for most of the past two thousand years. It springs from the biological, psychological, and social complementarity of the male and female sexes: Women typically bring to marriage important gifts and perspectives that men typically do not bring, just as men bring their own special gifts and perspectives that women typically cannot provide in the same way. This covenant of mutual dependence and obligation, solemnized by a legal oath, is strengthened by the pledge of permanence that husband and wife offer to one another—always to remain, never to flee, even and especially in the most difficult times.

## 2. Marriage is a profound human good, elevating and perfecting our social and sexual nature.

Human beings are social animals, and the social institution of marriage is a profound human good. It is a matrix of human relationships rooted in the spouses' sexual complementarity and procreative possibilities, and in children's need for sustained parental nurturance and support. It creates clear ties of begetting and belonging, ties of identity, kinship, and mutual interdependence and responsibility. These bonds of fidelity serve a crucial public purpose, and so it is necessary and proper for the state to recognize and encourage marriage in both law and public policy. Indeed, it is not surprising that marriage is publicly sanctioned and promoted in virtually every known society and often solemnized by religious and cultural rituals. Modern biological and social science only confirm the benefits of marriage as a human good consistent with our given nature as sexual and social beings.

## 3. Ordinarily, both men and women who marry are better off as a result.

Married men gain moral and personal discipline, a stable domestic life, and the opportunity to participate in the upbringing of their children. Married women gain stability and protection, acknowledgment of the paternity of their children, and shared responsibility and emotional support in the raising of their young. Together, both spouses gain from a normative commitment to the institution of marriage itself—including the benefits that come from faithfully fulfilling one's chosen duties as mother or father, husband or wife. Couples who share a moral commitment to marital permanency and fidelity tend to have better marriages. The marital ethic enjoining permanence, mutual fidelity, and care, as well as forbidding violence or sexual abuse, arises out of the core imperative of our marriage tradition: that men and women who marry pledge to love one another, "in sickness and in health" and "for better or for worse," ordinarily "until death do us part."

## 4. Marriage protects and promotes the well-being of children.

The family environment provided by marriage allows children to grow, mature, and flourish. It is a seedbed of sociability and virtue for the young, who learn from both their parents and their siblings. Specifically, the married family satisfies children's need to know their biological origins, connects them to both a mother and a father, establishes a framework of love for nurturing them, oversees their education and personal development, and anchors their identity as they learn to move about the larger world. These are not merely desirable goods, but *what we owe to children as vulnerable beings filled with potential.* Whenever humanly possible, children have a natural human right to know their mother and father, and mothers and fathers have a solemn obligation to love their children unconditionally.

## 5. Marriage sustains civil society and promotes the common good.

Civil society also benefits from a stable marital order. Families are themselves small societies, and the web of trust they establish across generations and between the spouses' original families are a key constituent of society as a whole. The network of relatives and in-laws that marriage creates and sustains is a key ingredient of the "social capital" that facilitates many kinds of beneficial civic associations and private groups. The virtues acquired within the family—generosity, self-sacrifice, trust, self-discipline—are crucial in every domain of social life. Children who grow up in broken families often fail to acquire these elemental habits of character. When marital breakdown or the failure to form marriages becomes widespread, society is harmed by a host of social pathologies, including increased poverty, mental illness, crime, illegal drug use, clinical depression, and suicide.

## 6. Marriage is a wealth-creating institution, increasing human and social capital.

The modern economy and modern democratic state depend upon families to produce the next generation of productive workers and taxpayers. This ongoing renewal of human capital is a crucial ingredient in the national economy, one that is now in grave peril in those societies with rapidly aging populations and below-replacement fertility rates. It is within families that young people develop stable patterns of work and self-reliance at the direction of their parents, and this training in turn provides the basis for developing useful skills and gaining a profession. More deeply, marriage realigns personal interests beyond the good of the present self, and thus reduces the tendency of individuals and groups to make rash or imprudent decisions that squander the inheritance of future generations. Families also provide networks of trust and capital that serve as the foundation for countless entrepreneurial small-business enterprises (as well as some large corporations), which are crucial to the vitality of the nation's economy. In addition, devoted spouses and grown children assist in caring for the sick and elderly, and maintain the solvency of pension and social-insurance programs by providing unremunerated care for their loved ones, paying taxes, and producing the children who will form future generations of tax-paying workers. Without flourishing families, in other words, the long-term health of the modern economy would be imperiled.

### 7. When marriage weakens, the equality gap widens, as children suffer from the disadvantages of growing up in homes without committed mothers and fathers.

Children whose parents fail to get and stay married are at an increased risk of poverty, dependency, substance abuse, educational failure, juvenile delinquency, early unwed pregnancy, and a host of other destructive behaviors. When whole families and neighborhoods become dominated by fatherless homes, these risks increase even further. The breakdown of marriage has hit the African-American community especially hard, and thus threatens the cherished American ideal of equality of opportunity by depriving adults and especially children of the social capital they need in order to flourish. Precisely because we seek to eliminate social disadvantages based upon race and class, we view the cultural, economic, and other barriers to strengthening marriage in poor neighborhoods—especially among those racial minorities with disproportionately high rates of family breakdown—as a serious problem to be solved with persistence, generosity, and ingenuity.

## 8. A functioning marriage culture serves to protect political liberty and foster limited government.

Strong, intact families stabilize the state and decrease the need for costly and intrusive bureaucratic social agencies. Families provide for their vulnerable members, produce new citizens with virtues such as loyalty and generosity, and engender concern for the common good. When families break down, crime and social disorder soar; the state must expand to reassert social control with intrusive policing, a sprawling prison system, coercive child-support enforcement, and court-directed family life.[3] Without stable families, personal liberty is thus imperiled as the state tries to fulfill through coercion those functions that families, at their best, fulfill through covenantal devotion.

## 9. The laws that govern marriage matter significantly.

Law and culture exhibit a dynamic relationship: changes in one ultimately yield changes in the other, and together law and culture structure the choices that individuals see as available, acceptable, and choice-worthy. Given the clear benefits of marriage, we believe that the state should not remain politically neutral, either in procedure or outcome, between marriage and various alternative family structures. Some have sought to redefine civil marriage as a private contract between two individuals regardless of sex, others as a binding union of any number of individuals, and still others as any kind of contractual arrangement for any length of time that is agreeable to any number of consenting adult parties. But in doing so a state would necessarily undermine the social norm which encourages marriage as historically understood—i.e., the sexually faithful union, intended for life, between one man and one woman, open to the begetting and rearing of children. The public goods uniquely provided by marriage are recognizable by reasonable persons, regardless of religious or secular worldview, and thus provide compelling reasons for reinforcing the existing marriage norm in law and public policy.

## 10. "Civil marriage" and "religious marriage" cannot be rigidly or completely divorced from one another.

Americans have always recognized the right of any person, religious or non-religious, to marry. While the ceremonial form of religious and secular marriages often differs, the meaning of such marriages within the social order has always been similar, which is why the state honors those marriages duly performed by religious authorities. Moreover, current social science evidence on religion and marital success affirms the wisdom of the American tradition, which has always recognized and acknowledged the positive role that religion plays in creating and sustaining marriage as a social institution.[4] The majority of Americans marry in religious institutions, and for many of these people a religious dimension suffuses the whole of family life and solemnizes the marriage vow. It is thus important to recognize the crucial role played by religious institutions in lending critical support for a sustainable marriage culture, on which the whole society depends. And it is important to preserve some shared idea of what marriage is that transcends the differences between religious and secular marriages and between marriages within our nation's many diverse religious traditions.

## III. EVIDENCE FROM THE SOCIAL AND BIOLOGICAL SCIENCES

In the last forty years, society has conducted a vast family experiment, and the outcomes are increasingly coming to light via scientific investigations. While no single study is definitive, and there is room at the edges for debate about particular consequences of marriage, the clear preponderance of the evidence shows that intact, married families are superior—for adults and especially for children—to alternative family arrangements. A great deal of research now exists from the anthropological, sociological, psychological, and economic sciences, demonstrating the empirical benefits of marriage.

In virtually every known human society, the institution of marriage has served and continues to serve three important public purposes. First, marriage is the institution through which societies seek to organize the bearing and rearing of children; it is particularly important in ensuring that children have the love and support of their father. Second, marriage provides direction, order, and stability to adult sexual unions and to their economic, social, and biological consequences. Third, marriage civilizes men, furnishing them with a sense of purpose, norms, and social status that orient their lives away from vice and toward virtue.[5] Marriage achieves its myriad purposes through both social and biological means that are not easily replicated by the various alternatives to marriage. When marriage is strong, children and adults both tend to flourish; when marriage breaks down, every element of society suffers.

## The Well-Being of Children

The evidence linking the health of marriage to the welfare of children is clear. During the last two decades, a large body of social scientific research has emerged indicating that children do best when reared by their mothers and fathers in a married, intact family. A recent report by Child Trends, a nonpartisan research organization, summarized the new scholarly consensus on marriage this way: "[R]esearch clearly demonstrates that family structure matters for children, and the family structure that helps children the most is a family headed by two biological parents in a low-conflict marriage."[6] Other recent reviews of the literature on marriage and the well-being of children, conducted by the Brookings Institution, the Woodrow Wilson School of Public and International Affairs at Princeton University, the Center for Law and Social Policy, and the Institute for American Values, have all come to similar conclusions.[7]

Marriage matters for children in myriad ways. We focus here on the educational, psychological, sexual, and behavioral consequences for children of family structure, beginning with education. Children reared in intact, married homes are significantly more likely to be involved in literacy activities (such as being read to by adults or learning to recognize letters) as preschool children, and to score higher in reading comprehension as fourth graders.[8] School-aged children are approximately 30 percent less likely to cut class, be tardy, or miss school altogether.[9] The cumulative effect of family structure on children's educational performance is most evident in high school graduation rates. Children reared in intact, married households are about twice as likely to graduate from high school, compared to children reared in single-parent or step-families. One study found that 37 percent of children born outside of marriage and 31 percent of children with divorced parents dropped out of high school, compared to 13 percent of children from intact families headed by a married mother and father.[10]

Marriage also plays a central role in fostering the emotional health of children. Children from stable, married families are significantly less likely to suffer from depression, anxiety, alcohol and drug abuse, and thoughts of suicide compared to children from divorced homes.[11] One recent study of the entire population of Swedish children found that Swedish boys and girls in two-parent homes were about 50 percent less likely to suffer from suicide attempts, alcohol and drug abuse, and serious psychiatric illnesses compared to children reared in single-parent homes.[12] A survey of the American literature on child well-being found that family structure was more consequential than poverty in predicting children's psychological and behavioral outcomes.[13] In general, children who are reared by their own married mothers and fathers are much more likely to confront the world with a sense of hope, self-confidence, and self-control than children raised without an intact, married family.

Marriage is also important in connecting children to their biological fathers and grounding their familial identities. Research by Yale psychiatrist Kyle Pruett suggests that children conceived by artificial reproductive technologies (ART) and reared with-out fathers have an unmet "hunger for an abiding paternal presence"; his research parallels findings from the literature on divorce and single-parenthood.[14] Pruett's work also suggests that children conceived by ART without known fathers have deep and disturbing questions about their biological and familial origins. These children do not know their fathers or their paternal kin, and they dislike living in a kind of biological and paternal limbo.[15] By contrast, children who are reared by their married biological parents are more likely to have a secure sense of their own biological origins and familial identity.

Family structure, particularly the presence of a biological father, also plays a key role in influencing the sexual development, activity, and welfare of young girls. Teenage girls who grow up with a single mother or a stepfather are significantly more likely to experience early menstruation and sexual development, compared to girls reared in homes headed by a married mother and father.[16] Partly as a consequence, girls reared in single-parent or step-families are much more likely to experience a teenage pregnancy and to have a child outside of wedlock than girls who are reared in an intact, married family.[17] One study found that only 5 percent of girls who grew up in an intact family got pregnant as teenagers, compared to 10 percent of girls whose fathers left after they turned six, and 35 percent of girls whose fathers left when they were preschoolers.[18] Research also suggests that girls are significantly more likely to be sexually abused if they are living outside of an intact, married home—in large part because girls have more contact with unrelated males if their mothers are unmarried, cohabiting, or residing in a stepfamily.[19]

Boys also benefit in unique ways from being reared within stable, married families. Research consistently finds that boys raised by their own fathers and mothers in an intact, married family are less likely to get in trouble than boys raised in other family situations. Boys raised outside of an intact family are more likely to have problems with aggression, attention deficit disorder, delinquency, and school suspensions, compared to boys raised in intact married families.[20] Some studies suggest that the negative behavioral consequences of marital breakdown are even more significant for boys than for girls. One study found that boys reared in single-parent and step-families were more than twice as likely to end up in prison, compared to boys reared in an intact family.[21] Clearly, stable marriage and paternal role models are crucial for keeping boys from self-destructive and socially destructive behavior.

Virtually all of the studies cited here control for socioeconomic, demographic, and even genetic factors that might otherwise distort the relationship between family structure and child well-being. So, for instance, the link between family breakdown and crime is not an artifact of poverty among single parents.[22] Moreover, the newest work on divorce follows adult twins and their children to separate out the unique effects of divorce itself from the potential role that genetic (and socioeconomic) factors might play in influencing children's outcomes. This research indicates that divorce has negative consequences for children's psychological and social welfare even after controlling for the genetic vulnerabilities of the parents who divorced.[23]

Why, then, does the evidence link marriage to an impressive array of positive outcomes for children? Both social and biological mechanisms seem to account for the value of an intact marriage in children's lives. From a sociological perspective, marriage allows families to benefit from shared labor within the household, income streams from two parents, and the economic resources of two sets of kin.[24] A married mom and dad typically invest more time, affection, and oversight into parenting than does a single parent; as importantly, they tend to monitor and improve the parenting of one another, augmenting one another's strengths, balancing one another's weaknesses, and reducing the risk that a child will be abused or neglected by an exhausted or angry parent.[25] The trust and commitment associated with marriage also give a man and a woman a sense that they have a future together, as well as a future with their children. This horizon of commitment, in turn, motivates them to invest practically, emotionally, and financially at higher levels in their children than cohabiting or single parents.[26]

Marriage is particularly important in binding fathers to their children. For men, marriage and fatherhood are a package deal. Because the father's role is more discretionary in our society (and every known human society) than the mother's role, it depends more on the normative expectations of and social supports provided to fathers by marriage. Marriage positions men to receive the regular encouragement, direction, and advice of the mother of his children, and encourages them to pay attention to that input.[27] Not surprisingly, cohabiting fathers are less practically and emotionally invested in their children than are married fathers.[28] Nonresidential fathers see their children much less often than do married, residential fathers, and their involvement is not consistently related to positive outcomes for children.[29] By contrast, married fathers can exercise an abiding, important, and positive influence on their children, and are especially likely to do so in a happy marriage.[30]

Biology also matters. Studies suggest that men and women bring different strengths to the parenting enterprise, and that the biological relatedness of parents to their children has important consequences for the young, especially girls. Although there is a good deal of overlap in the talents that mothers and fathers bring to parenting, the evidence also suggests that there are crucial sex differences in parenting. Mothers are more sensitive to the cries, words, and gestures of infants, toddlers, and adolescents, and, partly as a consequence, they are better at providing physical and emotional nurture to their children.[31] These special capacities of mothers seem to have deep biological underpinnings: during pregnancy and breast-feeding women experience high levels of the hormone peptide oxytocin, which fosters affiliative behaviors.[32]

Fathers excel when it comes to providing discipline, ensuring safety, and challenging their children to embrace life's opportunities and confront life's difficulties. The greater physical size and strength of most fathers, along with the pitch and inflection of their voice and the directive character of their speaking, give them an advantage when it comes to discipline, an advantage that is particularly evident with boys, who are more likely to comply with their fathers' than their mothers' discipline.[33] Likewise, fathers are more likely than mothers to encourage their children to tackle difficult tasks, endure hardship without yielding, and seek out novel experiences.[34] These paternal strengths also have deep biological underpinnings: fathers typically have higher levels of testosterone—a hormone associated with dominance and assertiveness—than do mothers.[35] Although the link between nature, nurture, and sex-specific parenting talents is undoubtedly complex, one cannot ignore the overwhelming evidence of sex differences in parenting —differences that marriage builds on to the advantage of children.

The biological relationship between parents and children also matters to the young. Studies suggest that biological parents invest more money and time in their offspring than do stepparents.[36] New research by University of Arizona psychologist Bruce Ellis also suggests that the physical presence of a biological father is important for the sexual development of girls. Specifically, he thinks that one reason that girls who live apart from their biological father develop sexually at an earlier age than girls who live with their biological father is that they are more likely to be exposed to the pheromones—biological chemicals that convey sexual information between persons—of unrelated males. He also finds that girls who are exposed to the presence of a mother's boyfriend or a stepfather reach puberty at an earlier age than girls who are raised by unpartnered single mothers.[37] There is clearly more research to be done in this area, but the data clearly suggest that one reason marriage is so valuable is that it helps to bind a child's biological parents to the child over the course of her life.

Sara McLanahan and Gary Sandefur, sociologists at Princeton and Wisconsin, respectively, sum up the reasons that marriage matters for children in this way: "If we were asked to design a system for making sure that children's basic needs were met, we would probably come up with something quite similar to the two-parent ideal. Such a design, in theory, would not only ensure that children had access to the time and money of two adults, it also would provide a system of checks and balances that promoted quality parenting. The fact that both parents have a *biological* connection to the child would increase the likelihood that the parents would identify with the child and be willing to sacrifice for that child, and it would reduce the likelihood that either parent would abuse the child."[38] Over the past few decades, we have experimented with various alternatives to marriage, and the evidence is now clear: children raised in married, intact families generally do better in every area of life than those raised in various alternative family structures. Those who care about the well-being of children—as every citizen should—should care about the health of modern marriage.

## The Well-Being of Adults

While the most important benefits of marriage redound to children, marriage also has significant benefits for the adult men and women who enter into it. Both married men and women benefit financially, emotionally, physically, and socially from marriage. However, we must also note that there are often gender differences in the benefits of marriage, and that the benefits of marriage for women are more sensitive to the quality of marriage than are the benefits of marriage for men.

The financial advantages of marriage are clear. Married men and women are more likely to accumulate wealth and to own a home than unmarried adults, even compared to similarly situated cohabiting or single adults.[39] Married men earn between 10 and 40 percent more money than single men with similar professional and educational backgrounds.[40] Married women generally do not experience a marriage premium in their earnings, but this is because most women combine marriage with motherhood, which tends to depress women's earnings.[41] The material benefits of marriage also extend to women from disadvantaged backgrounds, who are much less likely to fall into poverty if they get and stay married.[42] In general, marriage allows couples to pool resources and share labor within the household. The commitment associated with marriage provides couples with a long-term outlook that allows them to invest together in housing and other long-term assets.[43] The norms of adult maturity associated with marriage encourage adults to spend and save in a more responsible fashion.[44]

Marriage also promotes the physical and emotional health of men and women. Married adults have longer lives, less illness, greater happiness, and lower levels of depression and substance abuse than cohabiting and single adults. Spouses are more likely to encourage their partners to monitor their health and seek medical help if they are experiencing an illness.[45] The norms of adult maturity and fidelity associated with marriage encourage men and women to avoid unhealthy or risky behaviors, from promiscuous sex to heavy alcohol use.[46] The increased wealth and economic stability that come from being married enable married men and women to seek better medical care.[47] The emotional support furnished by most marriages reduces stress, and the stress hormones, that often cause ill health and mental illness.[48] Men are particularly apt to experience marriage-related gains in their life expectancy and overall health. Women also gain, but their marriage-related health benefits depend more on the quality of their marriages: women in low-quality marriages are more likely to experience health problems and psychological distress than single women, while good marriages give women an important psychological and physical boost.[49]

Marriage also plays a crucial role in civilizing men. Married men are less likely to commit a crime, to be sexually promiscuous or unfaithful to a longtime partner, or to drink to excess.[50] They also attend church more often, spend more time with kin (and less time with friends), and work longer hours.[51] One study, for instance, showed that only 4 percent of married men had been unfaithful in the past year, compared to 16 percent of cohabiting men and 37 percent of men in an ongoing sexual relationship with a woman.[52] Longitudinal research by University of Virginia sociologist Steven Nock suggests that these effects are not an artifact of selection but rather a direct consequence of marriage. Nock tracked men over time as they transitioned from singlehood to marriage and found that men's behaviors actually changed in the wake of a marriage: after tying the knot, men worked harder, attended fewer bars, increased their church attendance, and spent more time with family members.[53] For many men, marriage is a rite of passage that introduces them fully into an adult world of responsibility and self-control.

But why does marriage play such a crucial role in civilizing men—in making them harder workers, more faithful mates, and more peaceable citizens? Part of the answer is sociological. The norms of trust, fidelity, sacrifice, and providership associated with marriage give men clear directions about how they should act toward their wives and children—norms that are not clearly applicable to non-marital relationships. A married man also gains status in the eyes of his wife, her family, their friends, and the larger community when they signal their intentions and their maturity by marrying.[54] Most men seek to maintain their social status by abiding by society's norms; a society that honors marriage will produce men who honor their wives and care for their children.

Biology also matters. Research on men, marriage, and testosterone finds that married men—especially married men with children—have more modest levels of testosterone than do single men. (Cohabiting men also have lower levels of testosterone than single men.) Long-term, stable, procreative relationships moderate men's testosterone levels.[55] Judging by the literature on testosterone, this would in turn make men less inclined to aggressive, promiscuous, and otherwise risky behavior.[56]

Of course, marriage also matters in unique ways for women. When it comes to physical safety, married women are much less likely to be victims of violent crimes. For instance, a 1994 Justice Department report found that single and divorced women were more than four times more likely to be the victims of a violent crime, compared to married women.[57] Married women are also much less likely to be victimized by a partner than women in a cohabiting or sexually intimate dating relationship. One study found that 13 percent of cohabiting couples had arguments that got violent in the past year, compared to 4 percent of married couples.[58] Studies suggest that one reason women in non-marital relationships are more likely to be victimized is that these relationships have higher rates of infidelity, and infidelity invites serious conflict between partners.[59] For most women, therefore, marriage is a safe harbor.

It is not just marital status but the very ideal of marriage that matters. Married persons who value marriage for its own sake—who oppose cohabitation, who think that marriage is for life, and who believe that it is best for children to be reared by a father and a mother as husband and wife—are significantly more likely to experience high-quality marriages, compared to married persons who are less committed to the institution of marriage.[60] Men and women with a normative commitment to the ideal of marriage are also more likely to spend time with one another and to sacrifice for their relationship.[61] Other research indicates that such a commitment is particularly consequential for men: that is, men's devotion to their wife depends more on their normative commitment to the marriage ideal than does women's devotion to their husbands.[62] Simply put, men and women who marry for life are more likely to experience a happy marriage than men and women who marry "so long as they both shall love."

What is clear is that marriage improves the lives of those men and women who accept its obligations, especially those who seek the economic, emotional, and health benefits of modern life. Perhaps some modern men do not believe they need to be domesticated or do not wish to be burdened with the duties of child-rearing; and perhaps some modern women do not believe they need the security that a good marriage uniquely offers or fear that family life will interfere with their careers. But the data suggest that such desires can sometimes lead men and women astray, and that those who embrace marriage live happier lives than those who seek a false freedom in bachelorhood, cohabitation, or divorce.

## The Public Consequences of Marital Breakdown

The public consequences of the recent retreat from marriage are substantial. As the evidence shows, marital breakdown reduces the collective welfare of our children, strains our justice system, weakens civil society, and increases the size and scope of governmental power.

The numbers are indeed staggering. Every year in the United States, more than one million children see their parents divorce and 1.5 million children are born to unmarried mothers. The collective consequences of this family breakdown have been catastrophic, as demonstrated by myriad indicators of social well-being. Take child poverty. One recent Brookings survey indicates that the increase in child poverty in the United States since the 1970s is due almost entirely to declines in the percentage of children reared in married families, primarily because children in single-parent homes are much less likely to receive much material support from their fathers.[63]

Or take adolescent well-being. Penn State sociologist Paul Amato estimated how adolescents would fare if our society had the same percentage of two-parent biological families as it did in 1960. His research indicates that this nation's adolescents would have 1.2 million fewer school suspensions, 1 million fewer acts of delinquency or violence, 746,587 fewer repeated grades, and 71,413 fewer suicides.[64] Similar estimates could be done for the collective effect of family breakdown on teen pregnancy, depression, and high school dropout rates. The bottom line is this: children have paid a heavy price for adult failures to get and stay married.

Public safety and our justice system also have been affected by the retreat from marriage. Even though crime rates have fallen in recent years, the percentage of the population in jail has continued to rise: from .9 percent of the population in 1980 to 2.4 percent in 2003, which amounts to more than 2 million men and women.[65] Public expenditures on criminal justice—police, courts, and prisons—rose more than 350 percent in the last 20 years, from $36 billion in 1982 to $167 billion in 2001.[66] Empirical research on family and crime strongly suggests that crime is driven in part by the breakdown of marriage. George Akerlof, a Nobel laureate in economics, argues that the crime increase in the 1970s and 1980s was linked to declines in the marriage rate among young working-class and poor men.[67] Harvard sociologist Robert Sampson concludes from his research on urban crime that murder and robbery rates are closely linked to family structure. In his words: "Family structure is one of the strongest, if not the strongest, predictor of variations in urban violence across cities in the United States."[68] The close empirical connection between family breakdown and crime suggests that increased spending on crime-fighting, imprisonment, and criminal justice in the United States over the last 40 years is largely the direct or indirect consequence of marital breakdown.

Public spending on social services also has risen dramatically since the 1960s, in large part because of increases in divorce and illegitimacy. Estimates vary regarding the costs to the taxpayer of family breakdown, but they clearly run into the many billions of dollars. One Brookings study found that the retreat from marriage was associated with an increase of $229 billion in welfare expenditures from 1970 to 1996.[69] Another study found that local, state, and federal governments spend $33 billion per year on the direct and indirect costs of divorce—from family court costs to child support enforcement to Temporary Assistance for Needy Families (TANF) and Medicaid.[70] Increases in divorce also mean that family judges and child support enforcement agencies play a deeply intrusive role in the lives of adults and children affected by divorce, setting the terms for custody, child visitation, and child support for more than a million adults and children every year. Clearly, when the family fails to govern itself, government steps in to pick up the pieces.

The link between the size and scope of the state and the health of marriage as an institution is made even more visible by looking at trends outside the United States. Countries with high rates of illegitimacy and divorce, such as Sweden and Denmark, spend much more money on welfare expenditures, as a percentage of their GDP, than countries with relatively low rates of illegitimacy and divorce, such as Spain and Japan.[71] Although there has been no definitive comparative research on state expenditures and family structure, and despite that factors such as religion and political culture may confound this relationship, the correlation between the two is suggestive. Of course, we also suspect that the relationship between state size and family breakdown runs both ways. For instance, earlier research on Scandinavian countries by sociologists David Popenoe and Alan Wolfe suggests that increases in state spending are associated with declines in the strength of marriage and family.[72] Taken together, the retreat from marriage seems to go hand in hand with more expensive and more intrusive government; family breakdown goes hand in hand with growing hardship in disadvantaged communities, making the call for still more government intervention even more irresistible. It is a pathological spiral, one that only a restoration of marriage can hope to reverse.

## Four Threats to Marriage

Until forty years ago, marriage governed sex, procreation, and child-rearing for the vast majority of adults. In recent years, marriage's hold on these three domains of social life has weakened, with serious negative consequences for society as a whole. Four developments—the sad effect of decoupling marriage, sex, procreation, and child-bearing—are especially troubling: divorce, illegitimacy, cohabitation, and same-sex marriage.

***Divorce.*** From 1960 to 2000, the divorce rate more than doubled in the United States, from about 20 percent to about 45 percent of all first marriages. (Note: The divorce rate has declined modestly since 1980.) The data suggests that approximately two-thirds of all divorces involving children break up low-conflict marriages where domestic violence or emotional abuse is not a factor in the divorce.[73] Unfortunately, these children seem to bear the heaviest burden from the divorce of their parents.[74] Children from broken homes are significantly more likely to divorce as adults, to experience marital problems, to suffer from mental illness and delinquency, to drop out of high school, to have poor relationships with one or both parents, and to have difficulty committing themselves to a relationship.[75] Furthermore, in most respects, remarriage is no help to children of divorce. Children who grow up in stepfamilies experience about the same levels of educational failure, teenage pregnancy, and criminal activity as children who remain in a single-parent family after a divorce.[76]

Divorce is also associated with poverty, depression, substance abuse, and poor health among adults.[77] More broadly, widespread divorce poisons the larger culture of marriage, insofar as it sows distrust, insecurity, and a low-commitment mentality among married and unmarried adults.[78] Couples who take a permissive view of divorce are significantly less likely to invest themselves in their marriages and less likely to be happily married themselves.[79]

For all these reasons, divorce threatens marriage, hurts children, and has had dire consequences for the nation as a whole.

*Illegitimacy (non-marital child-bearing).* From 1960 to 2003, the percentage of children born out of wedlock rose from 5 to 35 percent.[80] Although growing numbers of children born out of wedlock are born into cohabiting unions—42 percent according to one recent estimate—most children born outside of marriage will spend the majority of their childhood in a single parent home, in part because the vast majority of cohabiting unions, even ones involving children, end in dissolution.[81] The biggest problem with illegitimacy is that it typically denies children the opportunity to have two parents who are committed daily to their emotional and material welfare.[82] As noted above, children raised in single-parent families without the benefit of a married mother and father are two to three times more likely to experience serious negative life outcomes such as imprisonment, depression, teenage pregnancy, and high school failure, compared to children from intact, married families—even after controlling for socioeconomic factors that might distort the relationship between family structure and child well-being.[83]

Non-marital child-bearing also has negative consequences for men and women. Women who bear children outside of marriage are significantly more likely to experience poverty, drop out of high school, and have difficulty finding a good marriage partner, even when compared to women from similar socioeconomic backgrounds.[84] Men who father children outside of marriage are significantly more likely to experience educational failure, earn less, and have difficulty finding a good marriage partner, even after controlling for socioeconomic factors.[85] Taken together, the rise of illegitimacy has been disastrous for children and adults, men and women, individuals and society.

*Cohabitation.* Since the early 1970s, cohabitation has increased more than nine-fold in the United States, from 523,000 couples in 1970 to five million in 2004.[86] Recent estimates suggest that 40 percent of children will spend some time growing up with one or both parents in a cohabiting union.[87] The growth of cohabitation in the United States is an unwelcome development. Adults in cohabiting unions face higher rates of domestic violence, sexual infidelity, and instability, compared to couples in marital unions.[88] Most studies find that cohabiting couples who go on to marry also face a higher risk of divorce, compared to couples who marry without cohabiting (although the risk of divorce for couples who only cohabit after an engagement does not appear to be higher than for married couples who did not cohabit).[89] Cohabiting unions are typically weaker than marriages, and appear more likely to lead to poor relationship outcomes. Cohabitation does not entail the same level of moral and legal commitment as marriage, couples often do not agree about the status of their relationship, and cohabiting couples do not receive as much social support from family and friends for their relationship as do married couples.[90]

Cohabiting unions are particularly risky for children. Children reared by cohabiting couples are more likely to engage in delinquent behavior, and be suspended from and cheat in school, compared to children reared by a married mother and father.[91] Children cohabiting with an unrelated adult male face dramatically higher risks of sexual or physical abuse, compared to children in intact, married families. For instance, one Missouri study found that preschool children living in households with unrelated adults (typically a mother's boyfriend) were nearly 50 times more likely to be killed than were children living with both biological parents.[92] Children also suffer from the instability associated with cohabiting unions. Even when children are born into cohabiting households headed by both their biological parents, they are likely to see one of their parents depart from the relationship. One recent study found that 50 percent of children born to cohabiting couples see their parents break up by their fifth year, compared to just 15 percent of children born to a marital union.[93] For all these reasons, cohabiting unions are not a good alternative to marriage but are a threat, and they surely do not provide a good environment for the rearing of children.

***Same-Sex Marriage.*** Although the social scientific research on same-sex marriage is in its infancy, there are a number of reasons to be concerned about the consequences of redefining marriage to include same-sex relationships. First, no one can definitively say at this point how children are affected by being reared by same-sex couples. The current research on children reared by them is inconclusive and underdeveloped—we do not yet have any large, long-term, longitudinal studies that can tell us much about how children are affected by being raised in a same-sex household.[94] Yet the larger empirical literature on child well-being suggests that the two sexes bring different talents to the parenting enterprise, and that children benefit from growing up with both biological parents. This strongly suggests that children reared by same-sex parents will experience greater difficulties with their identity, sexuality, attachments to kin, and marital prospects as adults, among other things. But until more research is available, the jury is still out.

Yet there remain even deeper concerns about the institutional consequences of same-sex marriage for marriage itself. Same-sex marriage would further undercut the idea that procreation is intrinsically connected to marriage. It would undermine the idea that children need both a mother and a father, further weakening the societal norm that men should take responsibility for the children they beget. Finally, same-sex marriage would likely corrode marital norms of sexual fidelity, since gay-marriage advocates and gay couples tend to downplay the importance of sexual fidelity in their definition of marriage. Surveys of men entering same-sex civil unions in Vermont indicate that 50 percent of them do not value sexual fidelity, and rates of sexual promiscuity are high among gay men.[95] For instance, Judith Stacey, professor of sociology at New York University and a leading advocate of gay marriage, hopes that same-sex marriage will promote a "pluralist expansion of the meaning, practice, and politics of family life in the United States" where "perhaps some might dare to question the dyadic limitations of Western marriage and seek some of the benefits of extended family life through small group marriages. . . ."[96]

Our concerns are only reinforced by the legalization of same-sex marriage in Belgium, Canada, the Netherlands, and Spain—and its legalization in the Commonwealth of Massachusetts. Same-sex marriage has taken hold in societies or regions with low rates of marriage and/or fertility.[97] For instance, Belgium, Canada, the Netherlands, Spain, and Massachusetts all have fertility rates well below the replacement level of 2.1 children per woman.[98] These are societies in which child-centered marriage has ceased to be the organizing principle of adult life. Seen in this light, same-sex marriage is both a consequence of and further stimulus to the abolition of marriage as the preferred vehicle for ordering sex, procreation, and child-rearing in the West. While there are surely many unknowns, what we do know suggests that embracing same-sex marriage would further weaken marriage itself at the very moment when it needs to be most strengthened.

# IV. ANALYSIS FROM POLITICAL AND MORAL PHILOSOPHY: THE INTRINSIC GOODS OF MARRIAGE

The empirical evidence in support of marriage is clear. When it comes to the myriad goods of modern social life—economic well-being, safety and security, personal happiness, flourishing community, limited government—marriage is a boon to adults and especially children. But the rational defense of marriage need not be based solely in data about its utility, and those who choose to marry are not usually motivated, first and foremost, by any utilitarian calculus. Only when marriage is valued as good in itself, and not simply as a means to other good ends, will children, adults, and societies reap its profound benefits. This requires defenders of marriage—teachers, poets, religious leaders, parents and grandparents, role models of every kind— to describe and defend why marriage is a choice-worthy way of life in terms that resonate with lived human experience. Some moral philosophers have engaged in extended reflection on the nature of marriage as a profound human good, seeking by precise analysis to better understand what most people accept as a matter of commonsense. Not all signatories to this statement accept this *natural law* approach or perspective, but we include it here since it represents a view that some thoughtful supporters of marriage find compelling.

Marriage offers men and women as spouses a good they can have in no other way: a mutual and complete giving of the self. This act of reciprocal self-giving is made solemn in a covenant of fidelity, a vow to stand by one another as husband and wife amid life's joys and sorrows, and to raise the children that may come as the fruit of this personal, sexual, and familial union. Marriage binds two individuals together for life, and binds them jointly to the next generation that will follow in their footsteps. Marriage elevates, orders, and at times constrains our natural desires to the higher moral end of fidelity and care.

The marriage vow by its nature includes permanence and exclusivity: a couple would lose the very good of the union they seek if they saw their marriage as temporary, or as open to similar sharing with others. What exactly would a temporary promise to love mean? Would it not reduce one's spouse to a source of pleasure for oneself, to be desired and kept only so long as one's own desires are fulfilled? By weakening the permanence of marriage, the contemporary culture of divorce undermines the act of self-giving that is the foundation of marriage. The marriage vow, seen as binding, is meant to secure some measure of certainty in the face of life's many unknowns—the certainty that this unknown future will be faced together until death separates. At the same time, marriage looks beyond the married couple themselves to their potential offspring, who secure the future from this generation to the next.

Marriage is thus by its nature sexual. It gives a unique unitive and procreative meaning to the sexual drive, distinguishing marriage from other close bonds. The emotional, spiritual, and psychological closeness of a married couple is realized in the unique biological unity that occurs between a man and a woman united as husband

and wife in sexual intercourse. In marital sexual union, the love of husband and wife is given concrete embodiment. Our bodies are not mere instruments. Our sexual selves are not mere genitalia. Male and female are made to relate to and complete one another, to find unity in complementarity and complementarity in sexual difference. The same sexual act that unites the spouses is also the act that creates new life. Sharing of lives is, in sex, also a potential sharing of life. In procreation, marital love finds its highest realization and expression. In the family, children find the safety, security, and support they need to reach their full potential, grounded in a public, prior commitment of mother and father to become one family together.

This deeper understanding of marriage is not narrowly religious. It is the articulation of certain universal truths about human experience, an account of the potential elevation of human nature in marriage that all human beings can rationally grasp. Many secular-minded couples desire these extraordinary things from marriage: a permanent and exclusive bond of love that unites men and women to each other and to their children.

But marriage cannot survive or flourish when the ideal of marriage is eviscerated. Radically different understandings of marriage, when given legal status, threaten to create a culture in which it is no longer possible for men and women to understand the unique goods that marriage embodies: the fidelity between men and women, united as potential mothers and fathers, bound to the children that the marital union might produce. Maintaining a culture that endorses the good of marriage is essential to ensuring that marriage serves the common good. And in a free society such as our own, a strong marriage culture also fosters liberty by encouraging adults to govern their own lives and rear their children responsibly.

As honest advocates of same-sex marriage have conceded, to abandon the conjugal conception of marriage—the idea of marriage as a union of sexually complementary spouses—eliminates any ground of principle for limiting the number of partners in a marriage to two. It would open the door to legalizing polygamy and polyamory (group marriage), and produce a culture in which marriage loses its significance and standing, with disastrous results for children begotten and reared in a world of post-marital chaos.

The law has a crucial place in sustaining this deeper understanding of marriage and its myriad human goods. The law is a teacher, instructing the young either that marriage is a reality in which people can choose to participate but whose contours individuals cannot remake at will, or teaching the young that marriage is a mere convention, so malleable that individuals, couples, or groups can choose to make of it whatever suits their desires, interests, or subjective goals of the moment.

Even as we defend the good of marriage as a way of life for individual men and women, therefore, we cannot ignore the culture and polity that sustain that way of life. Oxford University philosopher Joseph Raz, a self-described liberal, is rightly critical of those forms of liberalism which suppose that law and government can and should be neutral with respect to competing conceptions of moral goodness. As he put it:

> Monogamy, assuming that it is the only valuable form of marriage, cannot be practiced by an individual. It requires a culture which recognizes it, and which supports it through the public's attitude and through its formal institutions.[99]

Professor Raz's point is that if monogamy is indeed a key element in a sound understanding of marriage, this ideal needs to be preserved and promoted in law and in policy. The marriage culture cannot flourish in a society whose primary institutions, including universities, courts, legislatures, and religious institutions, not only fail to defend marriage but actually undermine it both conceptually and in practice. The young will never learn what it means to get married and stay married, to live in fidelity to the spouse they choose and the children they must care for, if the social world in which they come of age treats marriage as fungible or insignificant.

# V. AMERICAN EXCEPTIONALISM AND THE WAY FORWARD

When it comes to family life, the great paradox of our time is this: every society (including our own) that we think is generally best for human flourishing—stable, democratic, developed, and free—is experiencing a radical crisis around human generativity: enormous increases in family fragmentation and fatherlessness, usually coupled with the collapse of fertility to levels which, if continued, spell demographic and social decline. Suddenly, developed nations are finding themselves unable to accomplish the great, simple task that every human society must do: bring young men and women together to marry and raise the next generation together.

The United States has in some ways been the leader in this retreat from marriage, but in other ways (especially in recent years) has shown signs of unusual, renewed vitality. We are the only Western nation we know of with a "marriage movement."[100] We are the only large, developed nation to experience a sustained rise in fertility back to near-replacement levels.

The great task for American exceptionalism in our generation is to sustain and energize this movement for the renewal of marriage. We need to transmit a stronger, healthier, and more loving marriage culture to the next generation, so that each year more children are raised by their own mother and father united by a loving marriage, and so those children can grow up to have flourishing marriages themselves.

Creating such a marriage culture is not the job for government. Families, religious communities, and civic institutions, along with intellectual, moral, religious, and artistic leaders, need to point the way. *But law and public policy will either reinforce and support these goals or undermine them.* We call upon our nation's leaders, and our fellow citizens, to support public policies that strengthen marriage as a social institution. This nation must re-establish the normative understanding of marriage as the union of a man and a woman, intended for life, welcoming and raising together those children who are the fruit of their self-giving love, children who might aspire to marry and raise children of their own, renewing the life-cycle and extending the family tree from generation to generation.

In particular, we single out five areas for special attention:

1. **Protect the public understanding of marriage as the union of one man with one woman as husband and wife.**

   The law's understanding of marriage is powerful. Judges should not attempt to redefine marriage by imposing a new legal standard of what marriage means, or falsely declaring that our historic understanding of marriage as the union of one man and one woman is rooted in animus or unreason. Nor should the law send a false message to the next generation that marriage itself is irrelevant or secondary, by extending marriage benefits to couples or individuals who are not married.

   a. **Resist legislative attempts to create same-sex marriage; use legislative mechanisms to protect the institution of marriage** as a union of a male and a female as sexually complementary spouses. We urge our elected officials to support legislation that will properly define and promote a true conception of marriage. Likewise, we call on our elected representatives to vote against any bills that would deviate from this understanding of marriage. (We do not object to two or more persons, whether related or not, entering into legal contracts to own property together, share insurance, make medical decisions for one another, and so on.)

b. **End the court-created drive to create and impose same-sex marriage.** We call on courts directly to protect our understanding of marriage as the union of husband and wife. Radical judicial experiments that coercively alter the meaning of marriage are bound to make creating and sustaining a marriage culture more difficult, especially when such actions are manifestly against the will of the American people.

c. **Refuse to extend marital legal status to cohabiting couples.** Powerful intellectual institutions in family law, including the American Law Institute, have proposed that America follow the path of many European nations and Canada in easing or erasing the legal distinction between marriage and cohabitation. But we believe it is unjust as well as unwise to either (a) impose marital obligations on people who have not consented to them or (b) extend marital benefits to couples who are not married.

## 2. Investigate divorce law reforms.

Under America's current divorce system, courts today provide less protection for the marriage contract than they do for an ordinary business contract. Some of us support a return to a fault-based divorce system, others of us do not. But all of us recognize that the current system is a failure in both practical and moral terms, and deeply in need of reform. We call for renewed efforts to discover ways that law can strengthen marriage and reduce unnecessarily high rates of divorce. We affirm that protecting women and children from domestic violence is a critically important goal. But because both children and adults in non-marital unions are at vastly increased risk for both domestic violence and abuse, encouraging high rates of family fragmentation is not a good strategy for protecting women from violent men, or children from abusive homes.

Among the proposals we consider worthy of more consideration:

a. **Extend waiting periods for unilateral no-fault divorce.** Require couples in nonviolent marriages to attend (religious, secular, or public) counseling designed to resolve their differences and renew their marital vows.

b. **Permit the creation of prenuptial covenants that restrict divorce** for couples who seek more extensive marriage commitments than current law allows. (The enforcement by secular courts of Orthodox Jewish marriage contracts may provide a useful model.)

c. **Expand court-connected divorce education programs to include divorce interventions** (such as PAIRS or Retrouvaille) that help facilitate reconciliations as well as reducing acrimony and litigation.

d. **Apply standards of fault to the distribution of property, where consistent, with the best interests of children.** Spouses who are abusive or unfaithful should not share marital property equally with innocent spouses.

e. **Create pilot programs on marriage education and divorce interventions in high-risk communities,** using both faith-based and secular programs; track program effectiveness to establish "best practices" that could be replicated elsewhere.

## 3. End marriage penalties for low-income Americans.

To address the growing racial and class divisions in marriage, federal and state governments ought to act quickly to eliminate the marriage penalties embedded in means-tested welfare and tax policies—such as the Earned Income Tax Credit (EITC) and Medicaid—that affect couples with low and moderate incomes.[101] It is unconscionable that government levies substantial financial penalties on low-income parents who marry.

Other approaches to strengthening marriage for couples and communities at risk include public information campaigns, marriage education programs, and jobs programs for low-income couples who wish to get and stay married. Experimenting with such new initiatives allows scholars to determine which measures are best suited to the task at hand.[102]

## 4. Protect and expand pro-child and pro-family provisions in our tax code.

**5. Protect the interests of children from the fertility industry.**

Treating the making of babies as a business like any other is fundamentally inconsistent with the dignity of human persons and the fundamental needs of children. Among the proposals we urge Americans to consider, following in the footsteps of countries such as Italy and Sweden:

a. **Ban the use of anonymous sperm and egg donation for all adults.** Children have a right to know their biological origins. Adults have no right to strip children of this knowledge to satisfy their own desires for a family.

b. **Consider restricting reproductive technologies to married couples.**

c. **Refuse to create legally fatherless children.** Require men who are sperm donors (and/or clinics as their surrogates) to retain legal and financial responsibility for any children they create who lack a legal father.

The most important changes underwriting the current United States fertility industry are not technological; rather they are social and legal. Both law and culture have stressed the interests of adults to the exclusion of the needs and interests of children. Parents seeking children deserve our sympathy and support. But we ought not, in doing so, deliberately create an entire class of children who are deprived of their natural human right to know their own origins and their profound need for devoted mothers and fathers.

In sum, families, religious communities, community organizations, and public policymakers must work together toward a great goal:

strengthening marriage so that each year more children are raised by their own mother and father in loving, lasting marital unions. The future of the American experiment depends upon it. And our children deserve nothing less.

## NOTES

1.   Steven L. Nock. 2005. "Marriage as a Public Issue." *The Future of Children* 15: 13–32.

2.   W. Bradford Wilcox et al. 2005. *Why Marriage Matters, Second Edition: Twenty-Six Conclusions from the Social Sciences.* New York: Institute for American Values. Lorraine Blackman, Obie Clayton, Norval Glenn, Linda Malone-Colon, and Alex Roberts. 2005. *The Consequences of Marriage for African Americans: A Comprehensive Literature Review.* New York: Institute for American Values.

3.   David Popenoe. 1988. *Disturbing the Nest: Family Change and Decline in Modern Societies.* Aldine de Gruyter. Alan Wolfe. 1989. *Whose Keeper? Social Science and Moral Obligation.* Berkeley: University of California Press.

4.   www.law2.byu.edu/marriage_family/Charles%20Reid.pdf. W. Bradford Wilcox and Steven L. Nock. 2006. "What's Love Got to Do with It? Ideology, Equity, Gender, and Women's Marital Happiness." *Social Forces* 84: 1321–1345. Vaughn R. A. Call and Tim B. Heaton. 1997. "Religious Influence on Marital Stability." *Journal for the Scientific Study of Religion* 36: 382–392.

5.   W. Bradford Wilcox et al. 2005.

6.   Kristin Anderson Moore, Susan M. Jekielek, and Carol Emig, 2002. "Marriage from a Child's Perspective: How Does Family Structure Affect Children, and What Can Be Done About It?" *Research Brief, June 2002.* Washington, DC: Child Trends. P. 6.

7.     For summaries from Brookings and Princeton, see Sara McLanahan, Elisabeth Donahue, and Ron Haskins. 2005. "Introducing the Issue." *The Future of Children* 15: 3–12. For the Center for Law and Social Policy's statement, see Mary Parke. 2003. *Are Married Parents Really Better for Children?* Washington, DC: Center for Law and Social Policy. For the Institute for American Values' statement, see Wilcox et al. 2005.

8.     Elizabeth Marquardt. 2005a. *Family Structure and Children's Educational Outcomes.* New York: Institute for American Values.

9.     Ibid.

10.    Sara McLanahan and Gary Sandefur. 1994. *Growing Up with a Single Parent.* Cambridge: Harvard University Press.

11.    Wilcox et al. 2005. Elizabeth Marquardt. 2005b. *Between Two Worlds: The Inner Lives of Children of Divorce.* New York: Crown.

12.    Gunilla Ringback Weitoft, Anders Hjern, Bengt Haglund, and Mans Rosen. 2003. "Mortality, Severe Morbidity, and Injury in Children Living with Single Parents in Sweden: A Population-Based Study." *The Lancet* 361: 289–295.

13.    Sara McLanahan. 1997. "Parent Absence or Poverty: Which Matters More?" In G. Duncan and J. Brooks-Gunn, *Consequences of Growing Up Poor.* New York: Russell Sage.

14.    Kyle Pruett. 2000. *Fatherneed.* New York: Broadway. P. 207. See also Marquardt. 2005b and David Popenoe. 1996. *Life Without Father.* Cambridge: Harvard University Press.

15.    Pruett. 2000. Pp. 204–208.

16. Bruce Ellis. 2002. "Timing of Pubertal Maturation in Girls: An Integrated Life History Approach." *Psychology Bulletin* 130: 920–958.

17. McLanahan and Sandefur. 1994. Bruce Ellis et al. 2003. "Does Father Absence Place Daughters at Special Risk for Early Sexual Activity and Teenage Pregnancy?" *Child Development* 74: 801–821.

18. Ellis et al. 2003.

19. Wilcox et al. 2005.

20. Marquardt. 2005a. Paul Amato. 2005. "The Impact of Family Formation Change on the Cognitive, Social, and Emotional Well-Being of the Next Generation." *The Future of Children* 15: 75–96.

21. Cynthia Harper and Sara McLanahan. 2004. "Father Absence and Youth Incarceration." *Journal of Research on Adolescence* 14: 369–397.

22. Harper and McLanahan. 2004.

23. Brian D'Onofrio et al. 2006. "A Genetically Informed Study of the Processes Underlying the Association Between Parental Marital Instability and Offspring Adjustment." *Developmental Psychology*. Forthcoming. Brian D'Onofrio et al. 2005. "A Genetically Informed Study of Marital Instability and Its Association with Offspring Psychopathology." *Journal of Abnormal Psychology*. 114: 570–586.

24. Wilcox et al. 2005. McLanahan and Sandefur. 1994.

25. Wilcox et al. 2005. Popenoe. 1996.

26. Sandra Hofferth and Kermyt Anderson. 2003. "Are All Dads Equal? Biology Versus Marriage as a Basis for Paternal Involvement." *Journal of Marriage and Family* 65: 213–232. Wilcox et al. 2005.

27. Ross Parke. 1996. *Fatherhood*. Cambridge: Harvard University Press. P.101.

28. Hofferth and Anderson. 2003.

29. Valarie King and Holly Heard. 1999. "Nonresident Father Visitation, Parental Conflict, and Mother's Satisfaction: What's Best for Child Well-Being?" *Journal of Marriage and the Family* 61: 385–396. Elaine Sorenson and Chava Zibman. 2000. *To What Extent Do Children Benefit from Child Support?* Washington, DC: The Urban Institute.

30. Paul Amato. 1998. "More Than Money? Men's Contributions to Their Children's Lives." In Alan Booth and A. C. Crouter (Eds.), *Men in Families: When Do They Get Involved? What Difference Does It Make?* Mahwah, NJ: Lawrence Erlbaum Associates. Belsky, J.; Youngblade, L.; Rovine, M.; & Volling, B. 1991. Patterns of Marital Change and Parent-Child Interaction. *Journal of Marriage and the Family* 53: 487–498. Wilcox et al. 2005.

31. Eleanor Maccoby. 1998. *The Two Sexes: Growing Up Apart, Coming Together.* Cambridge: Harvard University.

32. David Geary. 1998. *Male, Female: The Evolution of Human Sex Differences*. Washington, DC: American Psychological Association. P. 104.

33. Wade Horn and Tom Sylvester. 2002. *Father Facts*. Gaithersburg, MD: National Fatherhood Initiative.

P. 153. Popenoe. 1996. P. 145. Thomas G. Powers et al. 1994. "Compliance and Self-Assertion: Young Children's Responses to Mothers Versus Fathers." *Developmental Psychology* 30: 980–989.

34. Pruett. 2000. Pp. 30–31. Popenoe. 1996. Pp. 144–145.

35. Geary. 1998. P. 142.

36. Anne Case et al. 2000. "How Hungry is the Selfish Gene?" *Economic Journal* 110: 781–804. Wilcox et al. 2005.

37. Bruce Ellis. 2002. "Of Fathers and Pheromones: Implications of Cohabitation for Daughters' Pubertal Timing." In A. Booth and A. Crouter (eds.) *Just Living Together: Implications of Cohabitation on Families, Children, and Social Policy*. Mahwah, NY: Lawrence Erlbaum Associates.

38. McLanahan and Sandefur. 1994. P. 38 (emphasis supplied).

39. Wilcox et al. 2005.

40. Wilcox et al. 2005.

41. Michelle J. Budig and Paula England. 2001. "The Wage Penalty for Motherhood." *American Sociological Review* 66: 204–225.

42. Wilcox et al. 2005.

43. Waite and Gallagher. 2000.

44. Ibid.

45. Ibid.

46. Ibid.

47. Ibid.

48. Ibid.

49. Wilcox et al. 2005. Daniel N. Hawkins and Alan Booth. 2005. "Unhappily Ever After: Effects of Long-Term Low-Quality Marriages on Well-Being." *Social Forces* 84: 451–472.

50. George Akerlof et al. Nock. 1998. Linda Waite and Maggie Gallagher. 2000. *The Case for Marriage*. New York: Doubleday.

51. Nock. 1998.

52. Waite and Gallagher. 2000.

53. Nock. 1998.

54. Nock. 1998.

55. Wilcox et al. 2005.

56. James Dabbs. 2000. *Heroes, Rogues, and Lovers: Testosterone and Behavior*. New York: McGraw-Hill.

57. Waite and Gallagher. 2000. p. 152.

58. Waite and Gallagher. P. 155.

59. Ibid.

60. Wilcox and Nock. 2006.

61. Ibid. Paul Amato and Stacy Rogers. 1999. "Do Attitudes Toward Divorce Affect Marital Quality?" *Journal of Family Issues* 20: 69–86.

62. Scott Stanley et al. 2004. "Maybe I do: Interpersonal commitment and premarital or nonmarital cohabitation." *Journal of Family Issues* 25: 496–519. Wilcox et al. 2005.

63. Adam Thomas and Isabel Sawhill. 2005. "For Love and Money? The Impact of Family Structure on Family Income." *The Future of Children* 15: 57–74.

64. Amato. 2005. p. 89.

65. Charles Murray. 2005. "The Hallmark of the Underclass." *Wall Street Journal* Sept. 29: A18.

66. www.ojp.usdoj.gov/bjs/glance/tables/exptyptab.htm.

67. George A. Akerlof. 1998. "Men Without Children." *The Economic Journal* 108: 287–309.

68. Robert J. Sampson. 1995. "Unemployment and Imbalanced Sex Ratios: Race Specific Consequences for Family Structure and Crime." In M. B. Tucker and C. Mitchell-Kernan (eds.). *The Decline in Marriage Among African Americans*. New York: Russell Sage. P. 249.

69. Isabel V. Sawhill. 1999. "Families at Risk." In H. Aaron and R. Reischauer, *Setting National Priorities: The 2000 Election and Beyond*. Washington: Brookings Institution.

70. David Schramm. 2003. *Preliminary Estimates of the Economic Consequences of Divorce*. Utah State University.

71. For family trends, see Timothy M. Smeeding, Daniel P. Moynihan, and Lee Rainwater. 2004. "The Challenge of Family System Changes for Research and Policy." In D. P. Moynihan, T. M. Smeding, and L. Rainwater (eds.), *The Future of the Family*. New York: Russell Sage. For information on state spending around the globe, see www.cia.gov/cia/publications/factbook/.

72. Popenoe. 1988. Wolfe. 1989.

73. Paul Amato and Alan Booth. 1997. *A Generation at Risk*. Cambridge: Harvard University Press.

74. Ibid.

75. Wilcox et al. 2005. Marquardt. 2005b. *Between Two Worlds*.

76. Wilcox et al. 2005. Sara McLanahan and Gary Qandefur. 1994. *Growing Up With a Single Parent: What Hurts, What Helps*. Cambridge: Harvard University Press.

77. Ibid.

78. Norval Glenn. 1996. "Values, Attitudes, and the State of American Marriages." In *Promises to Keep*, edited by D. Popenoe, J. Elshtain, and D. Blankenhorn. Lanham, MD: Rowman and Littlefield. Frank Furstenberg. 2001. "The Fading Dream: Prospects for Marriage in the Inner City." In *Problem of the Century*, edited by E. Anderson and D. Massey. New York: Russell Sage Foundation.

79. Wilcox et al. 2005.

80. David Popenoe and Barbara Dafoe Whitehead. 2005. *The State of Our Unions*. New Brunswick, NJ: National Marriage Project.

81. Timothy M. Smeeding, Daniel P. Moynihan, and Lee Rainwater. 2004. "The Challenge of Family System Changes for Research and Policy." In *The Future of the Family*, edited by D. Moynihan, T. Smeeding, and L. Rainwater . New York: Russell Sage Foundation. Popenoe and Whitehead. 2005. Wilcox et al. 2005.

82. Wilcox et al. 2005.

83. Wilcox et al. 2005.

84. Daniel Lichter. Daniel T. Lichter, Deborah Roempke Graefe, and J. Brian Brown. 2003. "Is Marriage a Panacea? Union Formation Among Economically Disadvantaged Unwed Mothers," *Social Problems* 50: 60–86. Daniel T. Lichter, Christie D. Batson, and J. Brian Brown. 2004. "Welfare Reform and Marriage Promotion: The Marital

Expectations and Desires of Single and Cohabiting Mothers." *Social Service Review* 38: 2–25. Lawrence L. Wu and Barbara Wolfe. 2001. *Out of Wedlock: Causes and Consequences of Nonmarital Fertility.* New York: Russell Sage Foundation.

85. Steven L. Nock. 1998. "The Consequences of Premarital Fatherhood," *American Sociological Review*, 63: 250–263.

86. Popenoe and Whitehead. 2005.

87. Larry Bumpass and Hsien-Hen Lu. 2000. "Trends in Cohabitation and Implications for Children's Family Contexts in the U.S.," *Population Studies* 54: 29–41.

88. Wilcox et al. 2005.

89. David Popenoe and Barbara Dafoe Whitehead. 2002. *Should We Live Together? What Young Adults Need to Know About Cohabitation Before Marriage: A Comprehensive Review of Recent Research.* New Brunswick, NJ: National Marriage Project.

90. Popenoe and Whitehead. 2002. Wilcox et al. 2005.

91. Wilcox et al. 2005.

92. Patricia G. Schnitzer and Bernard G. Ewigman. 2005. "Child Deaths Resulting from Inflicted Injuries: Household Risk Factors and Perpetrator Characteristics." *Pediatrics* 116: 6876–6893.

93. Wendy Manning, Pamela Smock, Debarum Majumdar. 2004. "The Relative Stability of Cohabiting and Marital Unions for Children." *Population Research and Policy Review* 23: 135–159.

94. Steven Nock. 2001. Affidavit to the Ontario Superior Court of Justice regarding Halpern et al. v. Canada.

Charlottesville, VA: University of Virginia Sociology Department. William Meezan and Jonathan Rauch. 2005. "Gay Marriage, Same-Sex Parenting, and America's Children." *Future of Children* 15: 97–115.

95. Esther Rothblum and Sondra Solomon. 2003. *Civil Unions in the State of Vermont: A Report on the First Year. University of Vermont Department of Psychology*. David McWhirter and Andrew Mattison. 1984. *The Male Couple*. Prentice Hall. Andrew Sullivan. 1995. *Virtually Normal*. New York: Knopf, first edition.

96. Judith Stacey. 1998. "Gay and Lesbian Families: Queer Like Us." In *All Our Families: New Policies for a New Century*, edited by M. A. Mason, A. Skolnick, and S. D. Sugarman. New York: Oxford University Press. Pp. 117, 128–129.

97. Council of Europe. 2004. *Recent Demographic Developments in Europe*. Strasbourg: Council of Europe Publishing. Daniel P. Moynihan, Timothy M. Smeeding, and Lee Rainwater. 2004. *The Future of the Family*. New York: Russell Sage Press.

98. Council of Europe. 2004. www.statcan.ca/Daily/English/050712/d050712a.htm. www.census.gov/population/projections/MethTab1.xls.

99. Joseph Raz, The Morality of Freedom (Oxford: Clarendon Press, 1986). P. 162.

100. www.americanvalues.org/pdfs/marriagemovement.pdf.

101. Adam Carasso and C. Eugene Steuerle. 2005. "The Hefty Penalty on Marriage Facing Many Households with Children." *The Future of Children* 15: 157–175.

102. Sara McLanahan, Elisabeth Donahue, and Ron Haskins. 2005. "Introducing the Issue." *The Future of Children* 15: 3–12.

## SIGNATORIES
[as of July 17, 2006]

M. Sophia Aguirre, Ph.D.
Associate Professor of
Economics, Catholic
University of America

Helen Alvare, J.D.
Associate Professor of Law,
Catholic University
Columbus School of Law

Hadley Arkes, Ph.D.
Ney Professor of
American Institutions
and Jurisprudence,
Amherst College

Herman Belz, Ph.D.
Professor of Constitutional
History, University of
Maryland at College Park

Louis Bolce, Ph.D.
Associate Professor of
Political Science,
Baruch College

Gerard Bradley, J.D.
Professor of Law, Notre
Dame Law School

Patrick Brennan, M.A., J.D.
Professor of Law and John F.
Scarpa Chair in Catholic
Legal Studies, Villanova
University School of Law

J. Budziszewski, Ph.D.
Professor of Government
and Philosophy,
University of Texas at Austin

James W. Ceaser, Ph.D.
Professor of Politics,
University of Virginia

Daniel Cere, Ph.D.
Director, Institute for the
Study of Marriage, Law, and
Culture, McGill University

Lloyd R. Cohen, Ph.D., J.D.
Professor of Law, George
Mason University School
of Law

John Coverdale, J.D., Ph.D.
Professor of Law, Seton Hall
University School of Law

Frederick C. DeCoste,
M.S.W., L.L.B., L.L.M.
Professor of Law,
University of Alberta
Faculty of Law

Dwight Duncan, J.D.
Professor of Law,
Southern New England
School of Law

David Eggebeen, Ph.D.
Associate Professor of
Human Development and
Sociology, Penn State
University

Jean Bethke Elshtain, Ph.D.
Laura Spelman Rockefeller
Professor of Social and
Political Ethics,
University of Chicago

Michael O. Emerson, Ph.D.
Allyn R. and Gladys M.
Cline Professor of Sociology
and Founding Director of
the Center on Race, Religion,
and Urban Life,
Rice University

Gene C. Fant, Jr., Ph.D.
Chair, Department of
English, Union University

Thomas E. Flanagan, Ph.D.
Professor of Political Science,
University of Calgary

David F. Forte, Ph.D., J.D.
Charles R. Emrick Jr.–Calfee,
Halter & Griswold Endowed
Professor of Law,
Cleveland-Marshall
College of Law

Elizabeth Fox-Geneovese, Ph.D.
Eléonore Raoul Professor of the Humanities and Professor of History, Emory University

Alfred J. Freddoso, Ph.D.
John and Jean Oesterle Professor of Thomistic Studies, University of Notre Dame

Jorge L. A. Garcia, Ph.D.
Professor of Philosophy, Boston College

Robert P. George, J.D., D.Phil.
McCormick Professor of Jurisprudence, Princeton University

Mary Ann Glendon, J.D., L.L.M.
Learned Hand Professor of Law, Harvard Law School

Alfonso Gomez-Lobo, Ph.D.
Ryan Family Professor of Metaphysics and Moral Philosophy, Georgetown University

Lino A. Graglia, L.L.B.
A. Dalton Cross Professor of Law, University of Texas at Austin

Earl L. Grinols, Ph.D.
Distinguished Professor of Economics, Hankamer School of Business, Baylor University

Anne Hendershott, Ph.D.
Professor of Sociology and Director of Urban Studies, University of San Diego

Joseph Horn, Ph.D.
Professor of Psychology, University of Texas at Austin

Robert Jenson, Ph.D.
Senior Scholar for Research,
Emeritus, Center for
Theological Inquiry,
Princeton, N.J., and Professor
of Theology Emeritus,
St. Olaf College

Byron Johnson, Ph.D.
Professor of Sociology,
Director, Center for
Religious Inquiry Across
the Disciplines,
Baylor University

Anthony M. Joseph, Ph.D.
Associate Professor of
History, Eastern University

Leon R. Kass, M.D., Ph.D.
Addie Clark Harding
Professor in the Committee
on Social Thought and the
College, University
of Chicago

Robert C. Koons, Ph.D.
Professor of Philosophy,
University of Texas at Austin

Peter Augustine Lawler,
Ph.D.
Dana Professor and Chair of
the Government Department
and International Studies,
Berry College

Wilfred M. McClay, Ph.D.
SunTrust Chair of Excellence
in Humanities and Professor
of History, University of
Tennessee at Chattanooga

Paul R. McHugh, M.D.
University Distinguished
Service Professor
of Psychiatry,
Johns Hopkins University
School of Medicine

Ralph McInerny, Ph.D.
Professor of Philosophy and
Michael P. Grace Professor of
Medieval Studies, University
of Notre Dame

Bruce M. Metzger, Ph.D.
George L. Collord Professor
Emeritus of New Testament
Language and Literature,
Princeton Theological
Seminary

Robert T. Miller, J.D.,
M.Phil.
Assistant Professor of Law,
Villanova University School
of Law

Jennifer Roback Morse,
Ph.D.
Senior Research Fellow
in Economics, The Acton
Institute for the Study of
Religion and Liberty

Russell K. Nieli, Ph.D.
Lecturer, Department of
Politics, Princeton University

Steven Nock, Ph.D.
Professor of Sociology and
Director of the Marriage
Matters Project, University of
Virginia

David Novak, M.H.L., Ph.D.
J. Richard and Dorothy Shiff
Professor of Jewish Studies,
University of Toronto

Marvin Olasky, Ph.D.
Professor of Journalism,
University of Texas at Austin

Michael Pakaluk, Ph.D.
Associate Professor of
Philosophy, Clark University

Alexander R. Pruss, Ph.D.
Associate Professor of
Philosophy, Georgetown
University

Jeremy Rabkin, Ph.D.
Professor of Government,
Cornell University

Steven E. Rhoads, Ph.D.
Professor of Politics,
University of Virginia

Daniel N. Robinson, Ph.D.
Philosophy Faculty,
Oxford University
Distinguished Research
Professor of Psychology,
Emeritus, Georgetown
University

Michael A. Scaperlanda, J.D.
Professor of Law and Gene
and Elaine Edwards Family
Chair in Law, The University
of Oklahoma College of Law

Roger Scruton, Ph.D.
Research Professor, Institute
for the Psychological Sciences

Gregory Sisk, J.D.
Professor of Law,
University of St. Thomas
School of Law, Minnesota

Katherine Shaw Spaht, J.D.
Jules F. and Frances L.
Landry Professor of Law,
Louisiana State University
Law Center

Richard J. Sperry, M.D.,
Ph.D.
Matheson Endowed Chair,
Health Policy
and Management,
University of Utah

Max L. Stackhouse, Ph.D.
Rimmer and Ruth de Vries
Professor of
Reformed Theology and
Public Life, Princeton
Theological Seminary

Richard Stith, J.D., Ph.D.
Professor of Law, Valparaiso
University School of Law

James R. Stoner, Jr., Ph.D.
Professor of Political Science,
Louisiana State University

Seana Sugrue, L.L.B.,
L.L.M., D.C.L.
Associate Professor of
Political Science,
Ave Maria University

Christopher O. Tollefsen, Ph.D.
Associate Professor of Philosophy, University of South Carolina

Michael Uhlmann, J.D., Ph.D.
Research Professor in Politics and Policy, Claremont Graduate University

Paul C. Vitz, Ph.D.
Senior Scholar, Institute for the Psychological Sciences
Professor Emeritus of Psychology, New York University

Lynn D. Wardle, J.D.
Bruce C. Hafen Professor of Law, Brigham Young University

Amy Wax, J.D., M.D.
Robert Mundheim Professor of Law, University of Pennsylvania Law School

Robert Louis Wilken, Ph.D.
William R. Keenan, Jr.
Professor of History, University of Virginia

Richard G. Wilkins, J.D.
Robert W. Barker
Professor of Law, Brigham Young University

James Q. Wilson, Ph.D.
Ronald Reagan Professor of Public Policy, Pepperdine University

Christopher Wolfe, Ph.D.
Professor of Political Science, Marquette University

Peter Wood, Ph.D.
Provost and Professor of Anthropology and the Humanities, The King's College

# A NOTE ON THE WITHERSPOON INSTITUTE

The Witherspoon Institute works to enhance public understanding of the political, moral, and philosophical principles of free and democratic societies. It also promotes the application of these principles to contemporary problems.

The Institute is named for John Witherspoon, a leading member of the Continental Congress, a signer of the Declaration of Independence, the sixth president of Princeton University, and a mentor to James Madison. As important as these and his other notable accomplishments are, however, it is Witherspoon's commitment to liberal education and his recognition of the dignity of human freedom, whether it be personal, political, or religious, that inspire the Institute's name.

In furtherance of its educational mission, the Witherspoon Institute supports a variety of scholarly activities. It sponsors research and teaching by means of a fellowship program; it sponsors conferences, lectures, and colloquia; and it encourages and assists scholarly collaboration among individuals sharing the Institute's interest in the foundations of a free society. The Witherspoon Institute also serves as a resource for the media and other organizations seeking comment on matters of concern to the Institute and its associated scholars.

For more information about the work of the Witherspoon Institute, please visit www.winst.org.